YOUR KNOWLEDGE HAS VALUE

Andreas Heiden

Using Social Media in Football Companies of the 1. Bundesliga

GRIN Verlag

Bibliografische Information der Deutschen Nationalbibliothek:

Die Deutsche Bibliothek verzeichnet diese Publikation in der Deutschen National-
bibliografie; detaillierte bibliografische Daten sind im Internet über http://dnb.d-
nb.de/ abrufbar.

Imprint:

Copyright © 2011 GRIN Verlag GmbH
Druck und Bindung: Books on Demand GmbH, Norderstedt Germany
ISBN: 978-3-656-62408-0

This book at GRIN:

http://www.grin.com/en/e-book/190677/using-social-media-in-football-companies-
of-the-1-bundesliga

Using Social Media in Football Companies of the 1. Bundesliga

Andreas Heiden

Field: Business English I

Table of contents

1. Introduction

Who thinks that football enterprises are only clubs is not right. Football clubs are even more big companies and its work has grown up. "Who thought that Bundesliga clubs only meet for a sporty competition should have a look into the companies register."(11 Freunde, P. 42, 2010) From the Bayern München AG to the St. Pauli Marketing GmbH, companies and professional trade have taken place in the Bundesliga.

The question is why does the Bundesliga need social media and why is social media a good instrument in the football business?

Football is probably the most popular sport in the world; about 174 million people in Europe are interested in it which makes about 71 percent. In Germany it is about 81 percent of the population. Because of this huge sympathy an economically coefficient grows out. (Comparative Sponsors, P. 32, 2009) Such loyal fans can bring more sales and the companies are not that forced to be successful in its sport. Football is also a European competition between clubs to get the best players, sponsors and the best sales. The clubs can influence the fans to buy more products or even attract new fans. A popular instrument to get attention and to get a better costumer relationship is using the social media.

2. Social Media

The term social media is a broadly defined and not clear defined term. Kaplan and Haenlein define social media as: "Social Media is a group of Internet-based applications that build on the ideological and technological foundations of Web 2.0, and that allows the creation and the exchange of User Generated Content."(Kaplan/Haenlein, P. 61, 2010)

Social Media is a synonym for Social Software. The software is in the form of web applications a free service offered for the users. The software is easily designed so that the user does not need any knowledge. (Comparative Adomeit, P.9,2008) The following functions are part of the social media and also offer users the possibility of active participation and generating content for the purposes of the community thought.

1. The *weblog* is a public diary or logbook. The blog is written by the Blogger regarding to his knowledge or impressions of a broad mass accessible. (Comparative

Töpfer/Silbermann/William,P.652, 2008) The term originated from the fact that the bloggers felt as the discoverer of the web, and so they write web logs (Blogs). The entries on a blog can and should be commented so that an interaction and an exchange between the viewers is possible. However, the default is always on the blogger core of the discussion, therefore, the blogger can control the course. The personality of the blogger also has a strong influence on the overall appearance and on the style of the blog. A blog is like a constantly updated journal, but there are far more options than the classic journalistic style offers. Any videos, radio shows, music etcetera can be put on a blog without much effort. (Comparative Weinberg, P.97ff, 2009) Technorati.com, a leading search engine for blogs, estimates the number of blogs worldwide to 133 million. (technorati.com, 2010) The totality of blogs is called blogosphere, proprietary blogs are called corporate blogs.

2. *Internet forums* are web pages that also include an opinion exchange. However, they offer other than the blog more freedom. In forums, registered users can start discussions, write comments and thus content is generated. Furthermore, discussions often extend over a longer period and are more structured. Comments to the same sub-themes are grouped into so-called "threads" and comments are displayed chronologically. Forums are often provided on homepages under the synonym community, to allow the user more participation. Forums are also used to collect complains as a part of the complaints management. (comparative Töpfer/Silbermann/William, P.654, 2008)

3. *Social networks* are large platforms. The content of social networks is the interaction, communication and networking of users. Social networks are popular sites on the internet. According to the website statistics service alexa.com, facebook.com is the second most popular website worldwide, only behind google.com. In Germany websites such as facebook, studivz/schülervz, xing and twitter are in the top 20 of the most visited websites. The social networks are based on profiles and offer ways to connect with like-minded in contact or build relations.

Twitter stands out a bit from the smorgasbord of social networks. On Twitter, it is less about user profiles, it is more about the answer to the question: "What are you doing?" This so-called micro-blogging service allows communicating within up to 140 characters of what users currently employs. Recipients of the status messages are "followers" that the status messages from particular users have subscribed so to speak. By keeping track of certain status messages of people, a networked community is formed. With the proliferation of mobile phones with broadband internet, Twitter has become popular because it is always possible to put news online. (Comparative Weinberg, P.141ff, 2009)

The profile on social networking sites like facebook, Xing or the VZnetworks gives information about the user, such as hobbies, education or general interests. This information can be consulted to find like-minded people and friends. With the help of friend invitations communities are formed. Most profiles are customizable and therefore give an accurate impression about the person. (Comparative Shuen, P.55, 2008) Most portals offer functions in order to protect privacy. However, in every community is a certain level of voluntary movement of users, who can in turn be used by companies to contact you. Messages and brands can be spread very well through social networks. Due to the strong networking and interacting profile sites of brands, products can be spread very quickly and increase their awareness. Using the example of facebook, which now is the largest social network and which was founded by Mark Zuckerberg in 2004. It is characterized by:

1. More than 600 million active user worlwide (in germany about 16 million users)

2. 50% of the users log on to facebook in any given day

3. Average user has 130 friends

4. People spend over 700 billion minutes per mounth on facebook

(comparative facebook statistic 2011)

These figures demonstrate the tremendous presence of facebook. Because facebook has so many features and for companies an enormous marketing potential, a steady growth is inevitable. (Comparative Weinberg, P.169, 2009) Facebook connects countless features to create their profile. In addition, it is easily possible, that not only private users have a profile; also brands, companies, music bands, actors, sport teams and football companies have profiles on facebook. Similar to a weblog you can create and upload videos, music or photos. This media can be relinked to other users. They are marked or linked on the used medium. The most important innovation is that it is similar to Twitter, a very high degree of topicality. News of friends are shown directly on your own profile. Through this function everybody is always up to date about the activities of their friends or favorite football club. The own profile is like a blog because status reports, long posts and all forms of media can be published. This information is sent to both, the friends and the related persons. At the same time facebook binds other sites such as YouTube or Twitter. Therefore these communities are not separated, they act together.

2.1. Online Communities in football

The represented communities and platforms which actually form a community will be presented with regard to the football.

The platform of the blogs, in form of corporate blogs, is a form which is rarely used. So there are various fan blogs that write about experiences and impressions of the favorite clubs, but not pure corporate blogs, so without the guidance of football companies.

More important are the internet forums of the various football clubs, because they are directly linked to the official website. It combines the function of a blog by published and commented videos or images. In addition, the convenient opportunity for discussions is given in the forum. Fans can register themselves and can be networked together to discuss about topics. This is striking that the customers/fans are involved through surveys or decisions.

Other strong and active communities in the football area are the communities of the football magazines such as Kicker and "11 Freunde". Both magazines are presenting a forum at their homepage, a fantasy league and football statistics on their own blog. These communities contribute the binding to the particular journal. But by a commitment to a brand or a particular football club, it cannot be assumed that an objective reporting or a balanced representation of all football clubs is provided.

The social networks have great potential to strengthen the brand, to win customers and to retain them. In February 2010 a study showed an enormous deficit of the Bundesliga clubs in the field of the social networks. (Comparative Sponsors, 2010) However, during the last year something has changed. The number of fans of the Bundesliga clubs on facebook is growing steadily, but in comparison with the top clubs from England or Spain there is still a significant gab.

Club	Fans on facebook March 2011
Bayern München (Germany)	920.439
Borussia Dortmund (Germany)	257.466
FC Barcelona (Spain)	10.544.578
Manchester United (England)	10.212.853
Inter Milan (Italy)	646.474
New York Red Bulls (USA)	510

(facebook.com, 10/03/2011)

There is a number of Bundesliga top clubs which have a very small number of fans on facebook (for example VfL Wolfsburg, SC Freiburg or Bayer Leverkusen). These Bundesliga clubs lose the opportunity to present themselves in a professional way.

2.2. Using Online Communities successfully

To maximize the chances of customer retention and minimize the risks, some points are important. Four of them will be explained shortly. (Comparative Tomczak/Schögel/Wentzel, P.534ff, 2006)

1. Avoid negative reputation
2. Support the growth of the community
3. Support the interaction of the members
4. Create a relevant added value

To *avoid negative reputation*, it is advisable to act credibly in particular. For this purpose, the creation of a community is not primarily intended as advertising. The users and customers must believe in the community and their personal benefit. (comparative Weinberg, P.342, 2009) The company should be interested in it too. Only when a functioning community is installed, the bond can be used. The community as such therefore has a higher priority than the spread through its marketing idea. A marketing campaign or an excessive commercialization of a community can lead to a negative image in the community. This negative image can be spread very quickly, so that damage for the company arises.

To support the growth of the community the following fact is evidenced: "The more members a community has, the more knowledge and resources can accumulate within the community and the more opportunities of individuals, in interaction with other members to resign." (Tomczak/Schögel/Wentzel, P.537, 2006) The community should be made popular. Banner ads on websites with regard to the facebook site, or regard in the newsletter can increase the popularity. In addition contests within the own community awareness increase the size of the community.

To *support the interaction of the members it is* required that the dissemination of content in any manner provides the necessary platforms. The company should therefore create forums, websites or blogs for the community, where members join and act interactively. The advantage of a facebook page is that the platform already exists and that it is only for a specific use, such as a football club to be modified. At the same time contents must be moderated and controlled, as well as interactive supportive measures such as surveys or games should be integrated. These tasks can be summarized in the management of the community. The purpose of a Community Manager is the maintenance and preparation of the content of the Community. (Comparative Weinberg, P.64 ff, 2009) The tasks of the establishment and maintenance of the community are to generate content of great importance. Therefore sufficient resources and knowledge should be found.

As a result of growth and the interactive community, *relevant added value* should be *created*. This added value to the individual user is from the fulfillment of its social needs such as contact, attention, integration and self-expression. In the form of a provision of a community the company should ensure that these targets are met. A large community can act confused. The individual can be lost in crowd which could affect the degree of his interaction. At the same time, the company should honor and value the community. The possibility of conversation/chat with a football star or the publication of exclusive news for community members gives the members the desired attention. By honoring active users in the form of articles in the blog or in the forums, their individual needs of self-expression will be satisfied. Knowing what the community what is essential. (Comparative Weinberg, P.47ff, 2009)

Besides the use of classical instruments, the communities provide new approaches for customer retention. In particular, the personal service and the social needs are emphasized. Therefore, customer retention, with the aid of communities, can be an important component for a comprehensive customer retention strategy of football business.

3. Conclusion

"Especially in the areas of brand management and customer loyalty, we benefit if customers use social media." (Stefan Mennerich, Head of New Media FC Bayern München, in Sponsors 2010) The paradigm shift, a shift from transaction marketing to relationship marketing with a focus on customer management, is provided. It is noted that a community for a club "[...] has a relatively personal way to communicate with fans and that they try to involve them into the club." (Stefan Mennerich, Head of New Media FC Bayern München, in Sponsors 2010)

The hope seems justified: In the area of the communities "[...] the fan can ask, answer, discuss, evaluate and recommend. The communication with his favorite club became a very special experience character and the bond to the brand is strengthened." (Sponsors, P.52, 2010) The control and initiation of communities in order to bind customers to a football business and to attract loyal and dedicated fans, is therefore worthwhile. Football firms should now deal with the issue further. A strategy must be worked out to integrate the customer relationship management into the whole company. For the coordination of the campaign it is advisable to establish a department or to appoint an agency. Customer retention should be applied consistently and sustainably; "snapshots" are usually not successful. The to-use platforms and their advantages are discussed. Thus, for example facebook have cost advantages and self-created communities have identification advantages, but the future expansion to multiple platforms is recommended. A look at the wider picture reveals that the potential is not exhausted. Foreign clubs have much more fans in its online communities than the clubs in the 1. Bundesliga.

Based on this work the trend is ignoring the issue customer loyalty no longer. Specifically, the online communities are a phenomenon which you cannot escape. To initiate a working community, one must believe in the community and ensure communication to the fore.

"If the community is only for the reason to sell something, the people notice this quickly and the community does not have the success they might have. If they want to participate because they make a real contribution to share their knowledge and to prove a service to the community, then they will sell it precisely to the right audience because they are so honest and sincere." (Weinberg, P.75,2009)

List of literature

11 Freunde (2010):
Bundesliga GmbH & Co.KG
In: 11 Freunde, August 2010, Nr. 105, P. 42-43.

Adomeit, S. (2008):
Kundenbindung im Web 2.0.
Hamburg: Diplomica Verlag 2008

Facebook statistics (2011):
Retrieved on 03/10/2011
http://www.facebook.com/#!/press/info.php?statistics

Facebook - Bayern München (2011):
Retrieved on 03/10/2011
http://www.facebook.com/FCBayern

Facebook - Borussia Dortmund (2011):
Retrieved on 03/10/2011
http://www.facebook.com/BVBorussiaDortmund09

Facebook – FC Barcelona (2011):
Retrieved on 03/10/2011
http://www.facebook.com/FCBarcelona

Facebook – Manchester United (2011):
Retrieved on 03/10/2011
http://www.facebook.com/ManchesterUnited

Facebook – Inter Milan (2011):
Retrieved on 03/10/2011
http://www.facebook.com/Inter-Milan

Facebook – Red Bull New York (2011):
Retrieved on 03/10/2011
http://www.facebook.com/NY-RedBulls

Kaplan, A. M./ Haenlein, M. (2010):
Users of the world, unite! The challenges and opportunities of Social Media
In: Business Horizons Vol.53, No. 1, (2010), S. 59-68.

Shuen, A. (2008):
Die Web 2.0 Strategie
Köln: O´Reilly.

Sponsors (2009):
Oediger, F.
Europa bleibt Fußballhochburg
In: Sponsors 08/2009 , P. 32

Sponsors (2010)
Bundesligisten nutzen Social Media zu wenig
Retrieved on 03/03/2011
http://www.sponsors.de/?id=71&no_cache=1&tx_ttnews[tt_news]=21176&tx_ttn
ews[backPid]=72

Technorati.com (2009):
State-of-the-blogosphere-introduction
Retrieved on 03/05/2011
http://technorati.com/blogging/article/state-of-the-blogosphere-introduction/

Tomczak, T./ Schögel, M./ Wentzel, D. (2006):
Communities als Herausforderung für das Direktmarketing
In: B. W. Burmann, Ganzheitliches Direktmarketing (P. 523-545).
Wiesbaden: GWV Fachverlage GmbH 2006

Töpfer, A./ Silbermann, S./ William, R. (2008):
Die Rolle des Web 2.0 im CRM.
In: A. Töpfer, Handbuch Kundenmanagement, P. 651-673.
Heidelberg: Springer Verlag 2008

Weinberg, T. (2009):
Social Media Marketing
Köln: O´Reilly Verlag 2009